BIBLE
BOOK OF BOOKS

GORDON MOORE

Ark House Press
arkhousepress.com

Cataloguing in Publication Data:
Title: Bible Book of Books
ISBN: 978-1-7636468-9-6 (pbk.)
Subjects: [REL006700]   RELIGION / Biblical Studies / Bible Study Guides;
[REL074000]   RELIGION / Christian Ministry / Pastoral Resources;
[REL067100]   RELIGION / Christian Theology / Soteriology;
Other Authors/Contributors: Moore, Gordon J

Published with Gordon J Moore
PO Box 46 Aspley Qld 4034 AUSTRALIA

"HEAVEN AND EARTH SHALL PASS AWAY, BUT MY WORD WILL NEVER PASS AWAY."

LORD JESUS CHRIST

Matthew 24:35

"Visit many good books, but live in the Bible"

C.H. Spurgeon
1834 - 1892

CONTENTS

INTRODUCTION

The Holy Bible is the 'book of books' that reveals the love affair God has with His human creation and declares salvation in the Lord Jesus Christ to all who will believe.

The Holy Bible has inspired, encouraged and strengthened millions of believers throughout the centuries.

The Holy Bible has guided nations in developing constitutions and judicial systems that have provided their citizens with freedom, justice, prosperity and peace. Such nations are described as 'Judeo-Christian' because their foundations are built upon the Bible.

The Holy Bible is still the #1 seller of all times because it captivates the human heart like no other book.

The Purposes of the Bible

The Holy Bible's spiritual qualities draw people to it again and again, filling the human heart with hope for eternity to come and giving direction and confidence in this mortal, present life.

The Holy Bible is the guiding light that the Holy Spirit uses to speak to us and guide us through our pilgrim journey of faith on earth.

> *"Your word is a lamp to my feet*
> *and a light to my path."*
> *Psalm 119:105*

The Holy Bible is the handbook and 'measuring rod' of the church, providing the pattern and the blue print for believers on how to work with Christ in building God's House.

The Holy Bible contains within its pages the "*instruction(s) in righteousness*" (2Timothy 3:16) for every believer in all aspects of life, both spiritually and practically, corporately and individually.

> *"His divine power has given to us all things*
> *that pertain to life and godliness,*
> *through the knowledge of Him who*
> *called us to glory and virtue,*
> *by which have been given to us exceedingly*
> *great and precious promises,*

> *that through these you may be*
> *partakers of the divine nature."*
> *2Peter 1:3*

The Holy Bible is the written Word of God, provided by God to leave us with no doubt regarding our salvation and eternal destiny in Christ.

> *"For we did not follow cunningly devised fables*
> *when we made known to you the power*
> *and coming of our Lord Jesus Christ,*
> *but were eyewitnesses of his majesty.*
> *For prophecy never came by the will of man,*
> *but holy men spoke as they were*
> *moved by the Holy Spirit."*
> *2Peter 1:16*

The Holy Bible equips us to be effective ministers of the Holy Spirit, bringing reconciliation to this lost world.

> *"From infancy, you have known*
> *the Holy Scriptures*
> *which are able to make you wise for*
> *salvation through faith, which is in*
> *Christ Jesus. Every Scripture is God-*
> *breathed and profitable for teaching,*
> *for reproof, for correction, and for*

instruction in righteousness,
that the man of God may be complete,
thoroughly equipped for every good work."
2Tim 3:15-17 (WEB)

Time for a 'New Reformation'

The 1517 Reformation occurred largely because the church of the day gradually departed from the teachings and doctrines of the Scriptures, which were either replaced by the doctrines of men or ignored completely.

We live in a similar era today.

Within Christendom there has been a gradual move over recent times away from following the teachings and doctrines of the Scriptures. Human opinions are becoming more important than God's Word as the western church is under assault from the secular, post-modern and liberal mindset.

Other forces are directly at work like the new 'left-progressive activists', of all political persuasions, who are relentlessly seeking to remove the Bible from everyday life. They view the Scriptures as containing "hate speech" that discriminates against minorities and lifestyles of all kinds.

However, the Bible is not "hate speech" at all, because "*God is love*" (1John 4:16). Rather, it is more accurate to state that the opponents of the Holy Bible hate what it speaks!

> *"I have given them Your word;*
> *and the world has hated them, because*
> *they are not of the world,*
> *even as I am not of the world."*
> *John 17:14*

Freedom of belief prosecutions

Cases are emerging in the USA, Canada and Europe where Christians are being prosecuted and fined by courts for exercising their constitutional religious freedoms to believe, quote and live according to the teachings and instructions of the Bible.

However, the saddest thing to observe is the gradual acceptance by many Christians of the post-modern, 'woke' doctrine and message of liberalism. The end result of this is the embracing of anti-Bible beliefs.

For many in Christendom the Holy Bible is becoming more and more irrelevant as the '*Rule of Faith*' for believers. The teachings and doctrines of the Holy Bible are being constantly deconstructed, reconstructed and redefined so as not to offend anybody in our 'politically correct' world.

> **"Our society strives to avoid any possibility of offending anyone - except God."**
> **Billy Graham**

A new day is dawning!

In the midst of these opposing voices, however, there is the sound of a new spiritual awakening occurring all over the world.

Christians are returning to the foundations of the faith and embracing once again the Holy Bible as the true and inspired Word of God in the midst of uncertainty, unbelief and fear.

> *"For this cause also thank we God*
> *without ceasing, because,*
> *when you received the word of*
> *God which you heard of us,*
> *you received it not as the word of men,*
> *but as it is in truth, the word of God,*
> *which effectually works also in you that believe."*
> *1Thessalonians 2:13*

Fresh revivals and moves of the Holy Spirit

Reports of revivals and fresh moves of the Holy Spirit in many nations are becoming a common occurrence.

The Holy Spirit is intensifying His activities to the nations in these last days of shaking and testing.

> *"Whose voice then shook the earth;*
> *but now He has promised, saying,*
> *Yet once more I shake not only*
> *the earth, but also heaven.*
> *Now this, Yet once more, indicates the*
> *removal of those things that are being shaken,*
> *as of things that are made, that the things*
> *which cannot be shaken may remain.*
> *Therefore, since we are receiving a*
> *kingdom which cannot be shaken,*
> *let us have grace, by which we*
> *may serve God acceptably*
> *with reverence and godly fear."*
> *Hebrews 12:26-28*

The Holy Scriptures are being returned to their rightful place; central to doctrine, life and practice for all true disciples of our Lord Jesus Christ.

The Church of Christ will rise to be the *"pillar and foundation (ground) of the truth"* in these last days before the imminent and visible return of the Lord Jesus Christ.

> *"So that you will know how people*
> *ought to conduct themselves*
> *in the household of God, which is*
> *the church of the living God,*
> *the pillar and foundation of the truth.*
> *1 Timothy 3:15 AMPLIFIED BIBLE*

My purpose in writing this book is to equip Christians with a greater understanding, acceptance and trust in the Bible, the Holy Scriptures. It is through the Holy Scriptures that we understand what salvation is so that we may experience it by faith in the Lord Jesus Christ.

> *"And that from childhood you have*
> *known the Holy Scriptures,*
> *which are able to make you wise for salvation*
> *through faith which is in Christ Jesus."*
> *2Timothy 3:15*

Dr Gordon Moore
AUTHOR

CHAPTER ONE

WHAT THE BIBLE SAYS
ABOUT ITSELF

The Holy Scriptures are the written Word of God, or *"logos"* in the Greek language, which are directly connected to the nature and character of God. Truthfulness is central to God's nature and character because He is truth. Therefore His Word is true because it is impossible for God to lie.

> *"…in which it impossible for God to lie"*
> Hebrews 6:18

The Bible stands alone as **'THE TRUTH'** given by God and therefore is self evident and needs no other support.

The Bible makes the following claims regarding itself.

The Bible is INSPIRED by God

*"All scripture is given by inspiration of God,
and is profitable for doctrine, for reproof, for
correction, for instruction in righteousness:
That the man of God may be perfect,
throughly furnished unto all good works."*
2Timothy 3:16

The Bible is ETERNAL

*"Heaven and earth shall pass away but
My Word will never pass away."*
Matthew 24:35

*"The grass withers, the flower fades,
but the word of our God will stand forever."*
Isaiah 40:8

The Bible is TRUE

*"Sanctify them through Your
truth: Your word is truth."*
John 17:17

'Inerrant' and 'infallible' are two theological concepts used to describe the truthfulness and reliability of the Bible.

"***Inerrant"*** means to be "***incapable of being wrong***"

(Oxford Dictionary) and "**infallible"** means to be "**incapable of making mistakes or being wrong**" (Oxford Dictionary). Therefore, the Holy Bible never seeks to prove itself to be true; it simply states itself to be so!

The Scriptures make numerous statements about its own pervasive truthfulness, such as:-

"The law of the Lord is perfect,
converting the soul:
the testimony of the Lord is sure,
making wise the simple.
The statutes of the Lord are
right, rejoicing the heart:
the commandment of the Lord is
pure, enlightening the eyes.
The fear of the Lord is clean, enduring for ever:
the judgments of the Lord are true
and righteous altogether."
Psalm 19:7-9

*"**The entirety of Your word is truth,***
and every one of Your righteous
judgments endures for ever."
Psalm 119:160 (Berea Standard Bible)

The Bible is POWERFUL

The Bible is God speaking to us in written form. Therefore, it is powerful and effective to fulfill God's purposes.

"For as the rain and the snow
come down from heaven
and do not return there but water the
earth, making it bring forth and sprout,
giving seed to the sower and bread to the eater,
so shall my word be that goes
out from my mouth;
it shall not return to me empty, but it
shall accomplish that which I purpose,
and shall succeed in the thing
for which I sent."
Isaiah 55:10-11 (English Standard Version)

The Bible is LIVING AND ACTIVE

The Bible cannot be viewed as any other book because it is *"God breathed"*. Therefore, God's words are alive and actively at work in the minds and hearts of any who would read and believe it.

*"**The word of God is alive and active**.*
Sharper than any double-edged sword,

it penetrates even to dividing soul
and spirit, joints and marrow;
it judges the thoughts and
attitudes of the heart."
Hebrews 4:12

The Bible is CHRIST CENTERED

The Bible has one central purpose: to declare the Lord Jesus Christ to the world.

"You study the Scriptures diligently because
you think that in them you have eternal life.
These are the very Scriptures
that testify about me,
yet you refuse to come to me to have life,
If you believed Moses, you would
believe me, for he wrote about me."
John 5:39-40

Jesus said to them, "How foolish you are,
and how slow to believe all that
the prophets have spoken!
Did not the Messiah have to suffer these
things and then enter his glory?"
And beginning with Moses and all the Prophets,

*He explained to them **what was said in all
the Scriptures concerning Himself**."*
Luke 24:25-27

When Jesus appeared to His disciples after His resurrection appearing He said to them:

"This is what I told you while I was still with you:
***Everything must be fulfilled that is
written about me in the Law of Moses,
the Prophets and the Psalms."***
*Then he opened their minds so they
could understand the Scriptures."*
Luke 24:44-45

The Bible is RELEVANT

The amazing thing about the Bible has been its ability to be relevant to every generation for thousands of years. This is because the message of the Bible transcends every culture, time and season.

*"Jesus answered, "It is written: 'Man
shall not live on bread alone,
but by every word that comes
from the mouth of God."*
Matthew 4:4

The Bible is REWARDING

The Bible promises to reward all who believe and obey it with life-long, fruitfulness and prosperity.

"Blessed is the man who does not walk
in the counsel of the ungodly,
nor stands in the way of sinners, nor
sits in the seat of the scornful.
But his delight is in the law of the Lord;
and in his law he meditates day and night.
And he shall be like a tree planted
by the rivers of water,
that brings forth his fruit in his season;
his leaf also shall not wither; and
whatever he does prosper."
Psalm 1:1-3

The Bible is GOD SPEAKING TO US

The Bible is very clear in declaring that we can trust what is written in it, because God is speaking directly to us through the Bible.

"For the word of God is alive, and powerful,
and sharper than any two-edged sword,

piercing even to the dividing asunder of soul and spirit, and of the joints and marrow, and is a discerner of the thoughts and intents of the heart."
Hebrews 4:12

CHAPTER TWO

JESUS AND THE SCRIPTURES

The Lord Jesus Christ displayed a remarkable knowledge and application of the Scriptures. He personally quoted the Old Testament 27 times as he preached and taught His gospel of the kingdom.

There are 180 Old Testament verses directly quoted and referred to in the four Gospels, with a further 283 quotations in the New Testament from the Hebrew Old Testament.

This is how significant the Scriptures were to the Lord Jesus Christ.

The Scriptures were central to the life and ministry of Jesus Christ. Not only did He recognize the need to obey the commands of Scripture, He also knew that He was fulfilling the Scriptures as the Messiah.

"Do not think that I have come to
destroy the law, or the prophets:
I have not come to destroy, but to fulfill."
Matthew 5:17

Jesus' confidence in the Scriptures

Jesus Christ placed His absolute trust and confidence in the Old Testament Scriptures because He knew He was the Incarnate Word of God and that the Scriptures were the written Word of God.

"For verily I say unto you, Till
heaven and earth pass,
one jot or one tittle shall in no wise
pass from the law, till all be fulfilled.
Whosoever therefore shall break one
of these least commandments,
and shall teach men so, he shall be called
the least in the kingdom of heaven:
but whosoever shall do and teach them,
the same shall be called great in
the kingdom of heaven.
For I say unto you, That except your
righteousness shall exceed the righteousness
of the scribes and Pharisees, ye shall in no
case enter into the kingdom of heaven."
Matthew 5:18-20

The Lord Jesus Christ knew that part of His mission was to inaugurate the writing of the New Testament through the inspiration and guidance of the coming Holy Spirit. This would be done through the 11 apostles and the apostle Paul.

The apostles are significant because they were:-

- **personally called, appointed and commanded** by Christ

- **eye witnesses** of Christ's ministry, miracles and resurrection

- **personally taught and trained** by Christ

- **entrusted** with the words, messages and teachings of Christ

- **appointed as the foundational leadership** of the church of Christ

It was through these apostles of Christ, and the apostle Paul, that the New Testament was written over the next 60 years and was completed in 90AD at the death of the last apostle, John.

Luke described this role in his introduction to his second book, The Acts of The Apostles:-

"The former treatise have I made, O Theophilus,
of all that Jesus began both to do and teach,
Until the day in which He was taken up,
after that He through the Holy Spirit
had given commandments to the
apostles whom He had chosen:
To whom also He showed Himself alive after
His passion by many infallible proofs,
being seen of them forty days,
and speaking of the things pertaining
to the kingdom of God."
Acts 1:1-3

This is why the Lord Jesus Christ personally authorized the Scriptures because they provide us with clarity and certainty about the will and purpose of God.

"All scripture is given by inspiration of God,
and is profitable for doctrine, for
reproof, for correction,
for instruction in righteousness."
2Timothy 3:16

Our confidence in the Scriptures

This absolute trust and confidence by Jesus Christ in the Scriptures presents us as believers with every reason to have the same level of trust and confidence in the Scriptures!

The apostle Peter declared that Jesus Christ ushered in the New Testament as *"a more sure word of prophecy"*. Therefore we can have absolute confidence and trust in it also.

"For we have not followed
cunningly devised fables,
when we made known unto you the power
and coming of our Lord Jesus Christ,
but we were eyewitnesses of His majesty.
For He received from God the
Father honor and glory,
when there came such a voice to
Him from the excellent glory,
This is my beloved Son, in
whom I am well pleased.
And this voice which came
from heaven we heard,
when we were with Him on the holy mount.
We have also a more sure word of prophecy;
whereunto ye do well that ye take heed,
as unto a light that shines in a dark place,
until the day dawn, and the day

star arise in your hearts:
Knowing this first, that no prophecy of the
scripture is of any private interpretation.
For the prophecy came not in old
time by the will of man:
but holy men of God spoke as they
were moved by the Holy Spirit."
2Peter 1:16-21

The birth of Jesus Christ

From the very beginning of the New Testament the birth
of Jesus Christ is announced as the fulfillment of the
prophecy of Isaiah.

"And she shall bring forth a son, and
you shall call His name JESUS:
for He will save His people from their sins.
So all this was done that it might be fulfilled
which was spoken by the Lord
through the prophet, saying:
"Behold, the virgin shall be with
child, and bear a son,
and they shall call His name Emmanuel",
which is translated, God with us."
Matthew 1:21-23

Jesus' temptation in the wilderness

We observe the total reliance and importance of the Scriptures by Jesus Christ at the beginning of His ministry in the temptation in the wilderness.

This sets the example for all disciples of Jesus to follow. Jesus Christ responded to every temptation of Satan by quoting the Word of God directly to him. This shows us that the Scriptures are the basis on which we are to live by faith and combat temptation.

First, when Satan tempted Jesus with food and appetite, Jesus quoted Deuteronomy 8:3; "**It is written**, *'Man shall not live by bread alone, but by every word that proceeds from the mouth of God.'"*(Matthew 4:4)

Second, when Satan tempted Jesus to test God and quoted the Scripture that He should jump from the pinnacle of the temple, Jesus quoted Deuteronomy 6:16: "**It is written again**, *'You shall not tempt the Lord your God.'"* (Matthew 4:7)

Third, when Satan offered Jesus the kingdoms of the world if He would worship him, Jesus rebuked Satan by quoting Deuteronomy 6:13, "Away with you, *Satan!* **For it is written**, *'You shall worship the Lord your God, and Him only you shall serve.'"* (Matthew 4:10)

The teachings of Jesus to fulfill the Scriptures

All through the Gospels the Lord Jesus Christ is found constantly quoting and referring to the Scriptures.

In His Sermon on the Mount, for example, in which Jesus Christ outlined the code of conduct for His kingdom, He repeatedly said, *"You have heard that it was said"* and then followed with, *"but I say to you"* (Matthew 5:21-22).

Jesus was not contradicting the Old Testament Scriptures, but rather He was introducing a whole new level of fulfilling the Scriptures by the power of the grace of God.

This was the direct opposite of merely obeying the Scriptures by the human effort of 'law keeping'!

> *"Think not that I am come to destroy*
> *the law, or the prophets:*
> *I am not come to destroy, **but to fulfill**."*
> *Matthew 5:17*

Jesus was calling His disciples to live above the righteousness of the scribes and Pharisees and to *"exceed"* them! This would happen because Jesus was inaugurating the life of faith through the grace of God. This was a 'Holy Spirit empowered life' that fulfilled the will of God from the heart.

"For I say to you, That unless your righteousness
exceeds *the righteousness of*
the scribes and Pharisees,
you will by no means enter into
the kingdom of heaven."
Matthew 5:20

An example of this 'new level' of living is found in Jesus' teaching in Matthew on murder and anger, in which the standard was above the act of murder. Jesus declared that His disciples would live above the temptation to murder by not even becoming angry "*without a cause*"!

"You have heard that it was said to
those of old, You shall not murder,
and whoever murders will be in
danger of the judgment.
But I say to you, That whoever is angry
with his brother without a cause
shall be in danger of the judgment.
And whoever says to his brother, Raca!
shall be in danger of the council.
But whoever says, You fool! shall
be in danger of hell fire."
Matthew 5:21

Jesus' two greatest commandments

When a lawyer tested Jesus by asking Him, *"Teacher, which is the great commandment in the Law."* Jesus replied by quoting Deuteronomy 6:5 and Leviticus 19:18.

> *"You shall love the Lord your*
> *God with all your heart,*
> *with all your soul and with all your mind.'*
> *This is the first and great commandment.*
> *And a second is like it:*
> *'You shall love your neighbour as yourself.'*
> *On these two commandments hang*
> *all the Law and the Prophets."*
> *Matthew 22:37-40*

Jesus' prayer and the Scriptures

In His prayer in John's gospel Jesus declared to His Father that He had fulfilled His ministry and given His disciples His Word.

> *"Now they have known that all things*
> *which You have Me are from You.*
> *For I have given to them the words*
> *which You have given Me;*
> *and they have received them, and have*
> *known surely that I came forth from You;*

and they have believed that You sent Me."
John 17:7-8

Jesus' crucifixion and resurrection and the Scriptures

At the end of Jesus' ministry when He is about to complete His assignment of redemption on the cross we see the Scriptures again being quoted and fulfilled in exacting detail.

First, when Judas betrayed Jesus for 30 pieces of silver and was buried by the priests in the *"Potter's Field"*, or *"Field of Blood"*, this was a fulfillment of the prophecy of Jeremiah.

"And they consulted together,
and bought with them the potter's
field, to bury strangers in.
Therefore that field has been called
the field of blood, to this day.
Then was fulfilled what was spoken
by Jeremiah the prophet*, saying,*
And they took the thirty pieces of silver,
the value of Him that was priced,
whom they of the children of Israel priced;
And gave them for the potter's field,
as the Lord directed me."
Matthew 27:7-10

Second, when Jesus was arrested He quoted Isaiah 53:12 which fulfilled the prophecy that Jesus would be counted as a criminal and a transgressor.

*"For I tell you that **this Scripture must be fulfilled in me**:*
'And He was numbered with the transgressors.'
For what is written about me has its fulfillment."
Luke 22:37

"Therefore I will divide Him a
portion with the many,
and He shall divide the spoil with the strong,
because He poured out his soul to death
and was numbered with the transgressors;
yet He bore the sin of many, and makes
intercession for the transgressors."
Isaiah 53:12

Third, on the cross at the point of death Jesus was mindful of the accomplishment of His mission and the fulfillment of the Scriptures.

"After this, Jesus knowing that all
things were now accomplished,
that the scripture might be
***fulfilled**, said, 'I thirst.'*

Now there was set a vessel full of vinegar:
and they filled a sponge with vinegar,
and put it upon hyssop, and put it to his mouth.
When Jesus therefore had received
the vinegar, he said, It is finished:
and bowing His head, He gave up His spirit."
John 19:28-30

This detail is described by David in his Psalm.

"They gave me also gall for my food;
and for my thirst they gave me vinegar to drink."
Psalm 69:21

Fourth, Jesus spoke the Scriptures in His final hours quoting the Psalm of David.

"And about the ninth hour Jesus
cried with a loud voice,
saying, Eli, Eli, lama sabachthani?
that is to say, My God, my God,
why have You forsaken me?"
Matthew 27:46

"My God, my God, why have You forsaken me?
why are You so far from helping me,
and from the words of my groaning?"
Psalm 22:1

"My strength is dried up like a potsherd;
and my tongue cleaves to my jaws;
and You have brought me into the dust of death.
For dogs have compassed me:
the assembly of the wicked have enclosed me:
they pierced my hands and my feet."
Psalm 22:15

When Jesus *"cried out with a loud voice, 'Father, into Your hands I commit My spirit.'"* (Luke 23:46), He was quoting Psalm 31:5.

Fifth, even after the death of Jesus Christ the Scriptures were fulfilled regarding the treatment of His body by the Romans. His bones were not broken, referring to Psalm 34:20, and they would piece His body, referring to Zechariah 12:10.

"Then came the soldiers, and
brake the legs of the first,
and of the other which was crucified with him.
But when they came to Jesus, and
saw that he was dead already,
they brake not his legs:
But one of the soldiers pierced
his side with a spear,
and immediately blood and water came out.

And he who has seen has testified,
and his testimony is true;
and he knows that he is telling the
truth, so that you may believe.
For these things were done that the
scripture should be fulfilled,
"Not one of His bones shall not be broken."
And again another scripture says, *"They*
shall look on Him whom they pierced."
John 19:33-37

Sixth, after His death, Jesus' clothes were bargained over by casting lots which was referring to in Psalm 22:18.

"They said therefore among themselves,
Let us not rend it, but cast lots
for it, whose it shall be:
that the scripture might be
fulfilled, *which says,*
They parted my raiment among them,
and for my vesture they did cast lots.
These things therefore the soldiers did."
John 19:24

Finally, after His death and burial, Jesus rose from the dead as Savior and Lord by the power of His Father. This fulfilled the prophecies of David and Isaiah.

"**For** *You wilt* **not leave** *my* **soul** *in Sheol,*
Nor will You allow Your Holy
One *to* **see corruption**."
Psalm 16:10

"*Yet it* **pleased** *the Lord to* **bruise** *Him;*
He has put him to **grief**, **when** *You*
make *His* **soul** *an offering for* **sin**,
He shall **see** *His* **seed**, *He shall*
prolong *His* **days**,
And the **pleasure** *of the Lord*
shall **prosper** *in His* **hand**."
Isaiah 53:10

After His resurrection, Jesus lived with His disciples for 40 days and was seen by many other witnesses before His ascension into heaven.

"**The former** *account I* **made**, **O Theophilus**,
of all that Jesus began both *to* **do and teach**,
Until the **day** *in* **which** *He was taken* **up**,
after He **through** *the Holy Spirit*
had given commandments to **the**
apostles whom *He had* **chosen**,
to whom He also presented Himself **alive**
after His suffering **by many** *infallible* **proofs**,
being **seen** *by* **them** *during* **forty days**,

and speaking *of the* **things pertaining**
to **the kingdom** *of* **God**.*"*
Acts 1:1-3

Time and space are insufficient to cover every Scripture regarding the birth, life, ministry, miracles, death, burial and resurrection of the Lord Jesus Christ. But they are recorded, revealing the high priority and importance of the Scriptures to Him.

CHAPTER THREE

THE ORIGINS AND RELIABILITY OF THE BIBLE

Where did the Bible come from? Is the Bible reliable? How did we get the English Bible?

To answer these questions and others like them we need to look into the origins of the Bible from history.

Origins and History

Over the centuries God has used two methods to provide for and protect the Holy Scriptures.

When I was in Prague, Czechoslovakia a few years ago on holidays with my wife, I observed the inscription on a government building next to the famous astronomical clock which caught my attention. It read; *"Providentia"* and *"Diligentia"*.

'**Providentia**' (providence) describes how God has acted sovereignly and providentially throughout history to provide us with the written Holy Scriptures.

'**Diligentia**' (diligence) describes how God has inspired men and women of faith to act diligently throughout history to record, copy, protect and preserve the Holy Scriptures.

> ### *GOD HAS GONE TO GREAT EFFORT AND COST OVER MANY CENTURIES TO PRESERVE THE HOLY SCRIPTURES FOR US*

Understanding the Reliability of the Bible

To understand the reliability of the Bible it is important to understand the three principles on which the Bible has been agreed upon, copied and translated:-

The '**Received Text**' - refers to the original text, original copies and ancient copies that have been preserved through the 'providence of God', which is God's desire and work to preserve the Scriptures. For example, we have much to thank the Roman Catholic Church for as they have faithfully preserved the original "*Vestus Latina*" (100-200AD) and the "Latin Vulgate Bible" (400AD) which was completed by Jerome. The Vulgate Bible was later translated into English in 1599, called the "Douay-Reims Bible", which we have available today.

Many of these original texts and copies are preserved in the Vatican Library and the British Museum

The '**Majority Text**' - refers to only what the majority of translators and scholars agree on. This comes from the legal concept of "*in the mouth of two or three witnesses let everything be established*".

The '**Bi-Partisan Text**' - refers to all Bible believing churches, denominations and groups who, although they may disagree on the specific interpretations of Scripture, accept the same and identical text based on the agreement of the 'Majority Text'.

We see the wonder of God's providence in using diametrically opposite translators, who never consulted with each other because they never knew one another, to all arrive at the same text!

These translations include:-

The **Vulgate** and **Douay-Rheims Bible** - Catholic

The **Geneva Bible** - Reformed

The **King James Bible** - Puritan

The **American Standard Version Bible** - Evangelical

The Geneva Bible and Vulgate Bible agree

"The Geneva Bible study notes contain some outspokenly anti-Roman Catholic content, as one might expect considering that Rome was still persecuting Protestants during it's development. Keep in mind that the English translators were exiles from England's Queen "Bloody" Mary who was burning Protestants at the stake while returning her nation to the Roman Catholic faith."
(Notes to the Modern Reader, 1599 Geneva Bible)

Evidence for Bible Manuscripts

The first step in establishing the credibility of the Bible is to consider the weight of evidence for the ancient manuscripts.

One of the arguments about the reliability of the Bible put forward by skeptics is that over the centuries major changes have occurred. However the evidence reveals that the ancient manuscripts have been reliably copied over the centuries, with most 'variations' being a matter of more accurately translating into other languages in order to keep the true meaning of the Scriptures.

So, how do we know that the ancient manuscripts have been copied reliably over the centuries?

There are basically three ways to know how the ancient manuscripts have been copied reliably over the centuries:

1. **Ancient Old Testament Manuscripts**

First, there exists **ancient, authoritative Old Testament manuscripts** such as the *Hebrew and* Aramaic *Masoretic Text* (800AD) and the *Greek Septuagint Text* (2nd Century BC).

When these two Old Testament texts are compared we find that they are 95% identical, despite being around 800-1000 years apart!

How accurate is the Masoretic Text?

*"Experts have been astonished at the fidelity of
the earliest printed version (late 15th century) to
the earliest surviving codices (late 9th century).
The Masoretic text is universally accepted as
the authentic Hebrew Bible.* (www.qesher.com)

The Dead Sea Scrolls (1947)

One of the greatest confirmations of the accuracy of the
Bible was the discovery of the *Dead Sea Scrolls* in 1947.

The *Dead Sea Scrolls* were most likely written by the
Essenes during the period from about 200 B.C. to 68 C.E./
A.D. and, most amazingly, are in substantial agreement
with the *Masoretic Text.*

These *"Dead Sea Scrolls,
provide a far older cross section
of scriptural tradition
than that available to scholars before."
(The Oxford Companion to Archaeology)*

Tens of Thousands of New Testament manuscripts

There are also **tens of thousands of New Testament
manuscripts** dating from the 2nd century AD to the
late 15th century. Furthermore, these manuscripts were

found scattered across Egypt, Palestine, Syria, Turkey, Greece and Italy making collusion unlikely.

Again, when these tens of thousands of texts are compared there are very few discrepancies!

2. Early Christian writings and Lectionaries

Secondly, there are a great number of **early Christian writings and Lectionaries** (books containing collections and portions of the Bible) from the first and second centuries that cite verses from the New Testament.

The quantity and scope of these citations make it possible to nearly write the whole New Testament from them!

Again, all these writings confirm the accuracy of the New Testament.

Examples of these writings and letters are:-

1. The Epistle of Clement to the Corinthians (95 AD)
2. The Letters of Ignatius to the churches in Asia Minor (115AD)
3. The Apology ("Defense") of Aristides of Athens to the Roman emperor, Antoninius Pius (125AD)

4.   The Epistle of Mathetes to Diognetus (130-200AD)

5.   "Against Heretics IV" by Irenaeus (168-176AD)

6.   "The Identity of the New Testament Text IV" by Tertullian (200AD)

7.   "Prescription Against Heretics" by Tertullian (200AD)

3. More evidence for Christian manuscripts

Thirdly, when we compare the manuscript evidence for ancient writings between Christian and non-Christian texts, we discover that "*there is substantially far more evidence for the existence and accuracy of Christian manuscripts.*" (Josh McDowell - josh.com)

Overwhelming number of Bible manuscripts

"All of the books of the New Testament were written within a lifetime of the death of Jesus of Nazareth. Not so the so-called "other gospels," which were pseudepigraphical Gnostic works written 100-300 years later. To date we have over 5800 Greek manuscripts of the New Testament, with an astounding 2.6 million pages of biblical text. While some of these manuscripts are small and

*fragmentary, the average size of a New
Testament manuscript is 450 pages.
Add to this the ancient manuscripts in Latin,
Coptic, Syriac, Armenian, etc. which number
in the tens of thousands, and you realize that
there is an embarrassment of riches when
it comes to New Testament manuscripts.
No other ancient text can compare with the New
Testament when it comes to the sheer volume
of manuscripts, nor when we consider how close
the earliest manuscripts are to the originals."*
(biblearcheologyreport.com)

What manuscripts of the ancient Bible do we have today?

We can be sure about the reliability of the Bible based on this one undeniable fact: "***there is an embarrassment of riches when it comes to New Testament manuscripts***." (biblearcheologyreport.com)

Ancient manuscripts

"Housed in the Sackler Library Papyrology Room at the University of Oxford, England are two of the earliest New Testament manuscripts.

According to the database maintained by the Center for the Study of New Testament Manuscripts (www.csntm.org), there are six other manuscripts that are also dated to the 2nd or 3rd centuries."

A Comparison of Ancient Works with the New Testament (Both Old and New Testaments)*

Numbers in () are previously reported dates.

Author	Work	Date Written	Earliest MSS	Time Gap	Old #	New
Homer	*Iliad*	800 BC	c.400 BC	400	643	1,800 +
Herodotus	*History*	480-425 BC	1st C AD	1,350	8	109
Sophocles	Plays	496-406 BC	3rd BC	100-200	100	193
Plato	Tetralogies	400 BC	895	1,300	7	210
Caeser	*Gallic Wars*	100-44 BC	9th C	950	10	251
Livy	*History of Rome*	59 BC - 17 AD	Early 5th C	400	1 Partial, 19	90 & 60 copies
Tacitus	*Annals*	100 AD	1st half: 850, 2nd: 1050 (1100 AD)	750-950	20	2 + 31 15 C copies
Pliny, the Elder	*Natural History*	49-79 AD	5th C frag: 1; Rem. 14-15th C	400 (750)	7	200
Thucydides	*History*	460-400 BC	3rd C BC (AD 900)	200 (1,350)	8	96
Demosthenes	Speeches	300 BC	Some frags from 1 C. BC. (AD 1100)	1,100 + (1,400)	200	340
Greek N.T. Manuscripts		500-100 AD	AD 130 (or less) [3]	50	5366	5,838
Greek New Testament Early Translations						18,524
Old Testament						42,000+**
Biblical Manuscripts, Scrolls and Translations;						
New Testament Greek Manuscripts						5,838
New Testament Early Translations						18,524
Old Testament Scrolls, Codices						42,000
TOTAL BIBLICAL MANUSCRIPT EVIDENCES						**66,362**

*All of these numbers can be obsolete by publication date
** The traditional listings of Old Testament manuscripts normally leave out all the abundant scroll evidence. It is not easy to determine the exact number of extant scrolls.

Some early copies of the New Testament in Greek. (Wikipedia list of Papyri)

To date there are over 140 papyri that are known.

Manuscript	Contents	Language	Date
Papyrus P32	Titus	Greek	2nd-3rd Century
Papyrus P46	Romans, 1 & 2 Corinthians, Galatians, Ephesians, Philippians, Colossians, 1 Thessalonians, Hebrews	Greek	2nd-early 3rd Century
Papyrus P66	Gospel of John	Greek	2nd-3rd Century
Papyrus P77	Gospel of Matthew	Greek	2nd-3rd Century
Papyrus P103	Gospel of Matthew	Greek	2nd-3rd Century
Majuscule GA0189	Acts of the Apostles	Greek	2nd-3rd Century

The 'Ancient Versions' of the Bible

1.   The **Vetus Latina ('Textus Receptus') -** a collective name given to **the 'received' Biblical texts written between 100-200AD** that were translated into Latin before Saint Jerome's '*Vulgate Bible*' in 382-405 AD. It became the standard 'Bible' for Latin speaking Western Christians. The phrase '*Vetus Latina*' is Latin for 'Old Latin' and the '*Vestus Latina*' is sometimes known as the '*Old Latin Bible*'.

2.   **The Septuagint** - the translation of the Hebrew Old Testament into Greek, made in Alexandria about **285BC**.

3.   **The Samaritan Pentateuch** - not strictly a version, but the Hebrew text perpetuated in Samaritan characters in around **122 BC**.

4.   **Peshito or Syriac** - the New Testament was translated around the **1st and 2nd century** with the whole Bible translated around the 5th Century. This is a translation into the common language of certain parts of Syria.

5.   **The Vulgate** - the whole Bible was translated into Latin by Jerome at Bethlehem, and completed in **405AD**. For over 1,000 years this was the standard Bible in the Roman Catholic Church. The first Catholic English Bible

was translated from the Vulgate in **1582AD** called the '***Douay-Rheims Bible***'.

The 'Most Ancient Copies'

Today we have many of the '***Most Ancient Copies***' made from the original manuscripts.

The three principle ones are:-

1.   The Codex Sinaiticus - written in the 4th Century and purchased from the Soviet Union in 1933 by Great Britain and is now in the British Museum.

2.   The Codex Alexandrinus - written in the 5th Century, now in the British Museum. It contains the whole Greek Bible with the exception of 40 lost leaves.

3.   The Codex Vaticanus - written around the 4th Century and is in the Vatican Library in Rome. It did contain the whole Bible but parts have been lost over the centuries.

(**SOURCE:** Thompson Chain Bible pages 180-181, No.4220)

The Formation of the 'Canon of Scripture'

It did not take long for the **Early Church Fathers (100-**

200AD) to recognize the need for a universally accepted '***Canon of Scripture***' in order to keep true to the teachings of the Lord Jesus Christ and the apostles.

> *"The term canon, from a Hebrew-Greek word*
> *meaning "cane" or "measuring rod,"*
> *passed into Christian usage*
> *to mean "**norm**" or "**rule of faith**."*
> *(britannica.com)*

The '*Canon of Scripture*', or the '*Holy Bible*', as we know it today, was established very early (100-200AD) as the standard or rule of measurement for all doctrine and practice in the church. This is known as the '*Rule of Faith*'.

Developments that forced the Church to establish a 'Canon'

Some of the reasons why a Canon of Scripture was established were:

- The need for a Scripture to spell out the message of Jesus Christ and the apostles

- The need to decide on what should be read in the churches

- The need for a 'true Canon' to answer heretical and counterfeit ones

- The need to establish 'Authoritative Truth' to answer error

- The need to decide which of many books claiming to be 'Canonical' were false

- The need to know which books to die for when possession resulted in martyrdom

The Development of the New Testament Canon

The 'Canon of Scripture', the 'Holy Bible', was accepted and authorized in **367AD** in the East, **382AD** in the West and finally accepted by the whole church in **397AD**.

The Popularity of the Bible

According to the Guinness World Records as of 1995, the Bible is the best-selling book of all time with an estimated **5 billion copies sold and distributed**.

The Origins and Growth of the English Bible

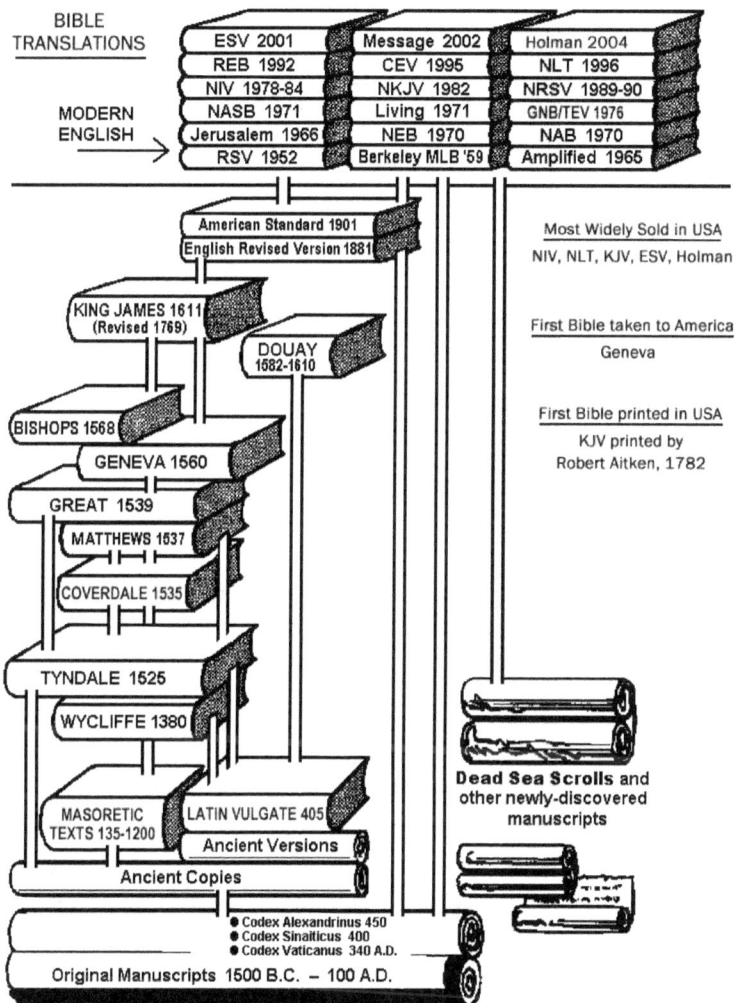

BIBLE TRANSLATIONS

MODERN ENGLISH →

ESV 2001	Message 2002	Holman 2004
REB 1992	CEV 1995	NLT 1996
NIV 1978-84	NKJV 1982	NRSV 1989-90
NASB 1971	Living 1971	GNB/TEV 1976
Jerusalem 1966	NEB 1970	NAB 1970
RSV 1952	Berkeley MLB '59	Amplified 1965

American Standard 1901
English Revised Version 1881

KING JAMES 1611
(Revised 1769)

DOUAY
1582-1610

BISHOPS 1568

GENEVA 1560

GREAT 1539

MATTHEWS 1537

COVERDALE 1535

TYNDALE 1525

WYCLIFFE 1380

MASORETIC TEXTS 135-1200

LATIN VULGATE 405

Ancient Versions

Ancient Copies

Dead Sea Scrolls and other newly-discovered manuscripts

● Codex Alexandrinus 450
● Codex Sinaiticus 400
● Codex Vaticanus 340 A.D.

Original Manuscripts 1500 B.C. – 100 A.D.

Most Widely Sold in USA

NIV, NLT, KJV, ESV, Holman

First Bible taken to America

Geneva

First Bible printed in USA

KJV printed by
Robert Aitken, 1782

Charted adapted, corrected and updated from Thompson Chain Reference Study Bible by David Ahl, 2015, www.BibleStudyMen.com

CHAPTER FOUR

THE CENTRALITY OF THE SCRIPTURES

*"All Scripture is inspired by God
and profitable for teaching, for reproof,
for correction, and for training in righteousness,
that the man of God may be complete,
equipped for every good work"*
2Tim. 3:16-17

The Reformers, led by prominent figures like John Calvin and John Knox and others, developed the concept of "***solar Scriptura***" which comes from the Latin to mean '*by Scripture alone*'.

This became known and widely accepted among Protestants and Evangelicals as the doctrine that holds that the Bible alone, or by itself, contains all knowledge and guidance necessary for salvation, holiness and the Christian life.

This Reformed doctrine concerning the Bible was in direct contrast to '***prima Scriptura***'; which was the doctrine held from the beginning of the church, and later by the Roman Catholic church.

The '*prima Scriptura*' view considers that besides, but not overriding, canonical Scripture, there are also other legitimate sources for a Christians belief, and hence how they are guided and should live.

Examples of these can include the general revelation in creation, charismatic gifts such as prophecy, spiritual insight and visions, angelic visitations, conscience, common sense, circumstances and experience, traditions and the views of experts such as leaders, pastors and bishops.

'*Sola Scriptura*' holds firmly to the view that any way of knowing or understanding God and His will that does not originate directly and solely from the canonized Scripture, are at best in a second place or largely ignored.

Some who hold this reformed position, especially in modern times, may accept that some of these 'secondary guidances' may be helpful, however, they are absolutely testable by the canon of Scripture and correctable by it.

The general outcome, therefore, is a suspicion and general rejection towards any guidance outside the Scriptures. This is because 'sola Scriptura' rejects any other authority other than the Bible. This was a direct reaction by the Reformers to the hierarchical Roman Catholic church at that time which they believed had strayed from a strict adherence to the Bible.

'Sola Scriptura' was and still remains a common and foundational doctrinal principle of Reformed and Evangelical churches today. Furthermore, it's effect down through the centuries is that most Bible-believing Christians today would agree that the Bible is authoritative because it's authority has been conferred by God. Thus, the Holy Scriptures are a divine instrument through which God communicates and reveals His will and authority.

The Roman Catholic Position of *'Prima Scriptura'*

The Catholic position on 'sola Scriptura' differs from most of Protestantism. The Roman Catholic Church believes that the Bible is inspired in the infallible original manuscripts. One of the main reasons that the Catholic has not accepted 'sola Scriptura' is due to the fact that there is no 'guide' to decipher important theological issues within the Church.

Therefore, the Roman Catholic church collected and organized the Holy Scriptures via tradition and has the Papal Office guiding and helping decipher important Scripture verses.

'Centrale Scriptura'; a modern centrist position

Most Bible-believing Christians in the Protestant world today, and especially Pentecostal and Spirit empowered Christians, would tend to hold a more 'centrist view' which we could call '***centrale Scriptura***'.

As with the Catholic position, '*centrale Scriptura*' accepts that God does speak through means other than the Bible. It holds to the belief that while the Scriptures are the supreme 'rule of faith' for all doctrine, life and practice, God does also speak in other ways to His people. These include general revelation in creation, traditions, charismatic gifts such as word of wisdom, word of knowledge, prophecy and teaching, spiritual insight, angelic visitations, conscience, common sense and the views of experts and leaders. All of these other ways are also subject to the need for 'interpretation' and 'guidance' by the church leadership where the Scriptures are not clear.

God has spoken in these Last Days in and through His Son

It is interesting to note that the Scriptures do declare that God has spoken in these "*Last Days*" in and through His Son, the Lord Jesus Christ, who is the the "*Living Word*" made flesh.

> *"God, who at various times and in various ways*
> *spoke in time past to the*
> *fathers by the prophets,*
> *has in these last days spoken to us by his Son…"*
> *Hebrews 1:1*

> *"In the beginning was the Word,*
> *and the Word was with God,*
> *and the Word was God.*
> *He was in the beginning with God."*
> *John 1:1-2*

The 'written Word', or the Scriptures, came between 33-90AD to record and confirm the life, ministry and teachings of Jesus Christ by the original apostles who were direct and authentic eyewitnesses of these. Later Paul was added because of his dramatic calling, conversion and revelation of the Gospel of the Grace of God (35-68AD).

"The former account have I made, O Theophilus,
of all that Jesus began both to do and teach,
Until the day in which he was taken up,
after that he through the Holy Spirit
had given commandments unto the
apostles whom he had chosen:
To whom also he shewed himself alive after
his passion by many infallible proofs,
being seen of them forty days,
and speaking of the things pertaining
to the kingdom of God."
Acts 1:1-3

"And I went up by revelation,
and communicated to them that gospel
which I preach among the Gentiles,
but privately to those who were of reputation,
lest by any means I might run,
or had run, in vain."
Galatians 2:2

Conclusion

When we ignore, dismiss, adjust, diminish or deny the Holy Scriptures when seeking to make decisions in matters of faith, doctrine, morality and life we will end up in deception, trouble and error. We will no longer be aligned with the Lord Jesus Christ and His living Word.

" Jesus answered them, "You are deceived,
because you don't know the Scriptures
or the power of God.»
Matthew 22:29

"For the Word that God speaks
is alive and full of power
[making it active, operative,
energizing, and effective];
it is sharper than any two-edged sword,
penetrating to the dividing line
of the *breath of life (soul)
and [the immortal] spirit, and
of joints and marrow
[of the deepest parts of our nature],
exposing and sifting and analyzing and judging
the very thoughts and purposes of the heart."
Hebrews 4:12 (Amplified Bible)

CHAPTER FIVE

THE NATURE OF THE BIBLE

"For the word of God is living and powerful,
and sharper than any two-edged sword,
piercing even to the division of soul and
spirit, and of joints and marrow,
and is a discerner of the thoughts
and intents of the heart."
Hebrews 4:12

The Power of the Word of God

The Bible declares that it is *"living and powerful"* (Hebrews 4:12). In other words, it is eternal and lives forever; it is full of power and vigor, it is strong and it is effectual.

"Heaven and earth will pass away, but
My words will not pass away."
Matthew 24:35

The Amplified Bible translates this statement in Hebrews 4:12 as being *"Full of power making it active, operative, energizing and effective"*.

GOD'S WORD IS DIFFERENT
THAN ANY OTHER WORD

God's word is different to any other word because God *"breathes His Word"*; this is what makes the Scriptures alive, powerful and effective.

"Every Scripture is God-breathed…"
2Timothy 3:16

Furthermore, the Word of God is effective because God is personally *"watching over His Word to perform it"* (Jeremiah1:13 WEB). This causes the Scriptures to not only be infallible but also unstoppable! In other words, God's Word will accomplish exactly what it was spoken to perform.

"So shall my word be that goes
forth out of my mouth:
it shall not return to me void, but it
will accomplish what I please,
and it shall prosper in the thing
for which I sent it."
Isaiah 55:11

The Word of God works deep in our lives

The writer to the Hebrews likens the Word of God to a sword that is *"sharper than any two-edged sword"*.

This is because the word of God divides between the soul and spirit and even pierces through the physical nature of man - to the very core of humanity!

The Amplified Bible describes this as a penetration *"of the deepest parts of our nature."*

The Bible judges our thoughts and motives

As we read the Bible it begins to discern, expose and judge our innermost thoughts and intentions as the light of God.

> *"For the word of God is living and*
> *active and full of power*
> *[making it operative, energizing, and effective].*
> *It is sharper than any two-edged sword,*
> *penetrating as far as the division*
> *of the soul and spirit*
> *[the completeness of a person],*
> *and of both joints and marrow [the*
> *deepest parts of our nature],*

exposing and judging the very thoughts
and intentions of the heart."
Hebrews 4:11 Amplified Bible

The cleansing power of the Bible

After the Bible has exposed and revealed our sins, evil thoughts, motives and intentions to us, it begins to cleanse us and fill us with faith, godly thoughts and intentions.

We are made clean by the word of God.

"Now you are clean through the word
that I have spoken to you."
John 15:3

In His prayer for his disciples, Jesus termed this cleansing by His words as a "sanctifying work". To sanctify means to cleanse and separate someone or something to God.

The Word of God separates us to God as we receive it and obey it by faith.

"Sanctify them through Your
truth: Your word is truth."
John 17:17

The mirror effect of the Bible

As the believer constantly "*beholds*", or looks at the Word of God, the glory, nature and image of God begins to reflect like a mirror on their face and in their heart.

The Bible is God's inspired instrument of change and transformation. The Holy Spirit inspires the Word of God in our hearts as we read it, giving us revelation and understanding that transforms us.

> *"But we all, with unveiled face beholding*
> *as in a mirror the glory of the Lord,*
> *are transformed into the same*
> *image from glory to glory,*
> *even as from the Lord, the Spirit."*
> *2Corinthians 3:18*

12 Symbols of the Word of God

The following 12 symbols of the Word of God helps us understand it's true nature and power.

1. A FIRE TO REFINE

> *"Is not my word like as a fire? says the Lord…"*
> *Jeremiah 23:29*

2. A HAMMER TO BREAK THE ROCK

*"and like a hammer that breaks
the rock in pieces?
Jeremiah 23:29*

3. A MIRROR TO REFLECT AND TRANSFORM

*"For if anyone is a hearer of the
word and not a doer,
he is like a man observing his
natural face in a mirror;
For he observes himself, goes away,
and immediately forgets what
kind of man he was.
But he who looks into the perfect law
of liberty, and continues in it,
and is not a forgetful hearer
but a doer of the work,
this one will be blessed in what he does."
James 1:23-25*

4. A SEED TO ENDURE FOREVER

*"Having been born again, not of
corruptible seed but of incorruptible,*

*through the word of God, which
lives and abides for ever.
because "All flesh is as grass, and all the
glory of man as the flower of the grass.
The grass withers, and its flower falls away,
But the word of the Lord endures for ever."
Now this is the word which by the
gospel was preached to you."
1Peter 1:23-25*

5. A LAVER TO CLEANSE

*"That He might sanctify and cleanse her
with the washing of water by the word."
Ephesians 5:26*

6. A LAMP TO GUIDE

*"Your word is a lamp to my feet,
and a light to my path."
Psalm 119:105*

7. RAIN AND SNOW TO REFRESH

*"For as the rain comes down and
the snow from heaven,*

And do not return there, but water the earth,
and make it bring forth and bud,
that it may give seed to the sower,
and bread to the eater,
So shall my word be that goes
forth out of my mouth:
it shall not return to me void, but it
will accomplish what I please,
and it shall prosper in the thing
for which I sent it."
Isaiah 55:11

8. A SWORD to PIERCE and DIVIDE

"For the word of God is living and
active and full of power
[making it operative, energizing, and effective].
It is sharper than any two-edged sword,
penetrating as far as the division
of the soul and spirit
[the completeness of a person],
and of both joints and marrow [the
deepest parts of our nature],
exposing and judging the very thoughts
and intentions of the heart."
Hebrews 4:12 Amplified Bible

10. GOLD to ENRICH

"The law of the Lord is perfect,
converting the soul:
the testimony of the Lord is sure,
making wise the simple.
The statutes of the Lord are
right, rejoicing the heart:
the commandment of the Lord is
pure, enlightening the eyes.
The fear of the Lord is clean, enduring for ever:
the judgments of the Lord are true
and righteous altogether.
More to be desired are they than
gold, yes, than much fine gold…"
Psalm 19:7-10

11. POWER to CREATE FAITH

"So then faith comes by hearing,
and hearing by the Word of God."
Rom 10:17

12. FOOD to NOURISH

a. *MILK for BABES*

> *"As newborn babes, desire the*
> *sincere milk of the word,*
> *that you may grow thereby."*
> *1Peter 2:2*

b. *BREAD for the HUNGRY*

> *"But He answered and said, It is written,*
> *Man shall not live by bread alone,*
> *but by every word that proceeds*
> *out of the mouth of God."*
> *Matthew 4:4*

c. *MEAT for MATURE ONES*

> *"For when for the time you*
> *ought to be teachers,*
> *you have need of one to teach you again*
> *the first principles of the oracles of God;*
> *and have become such as need of*
> *milk, and not strong meat.*
> *For every one that uses milk is unskilful in the*

word of righteousness: for he is a babe.
But strong meat belongs to
them who are of full age,
even those who by reason of use
have their senses exercised
to discern both good and evil."
Hebrews 5:11-14

d. **HONEY for DESSERT**

"More to be desired are they than
gold, yes, than much fine gold:
sweeter also than honey and the honeycomb."
Psalm 19:10

CHAPTER SIX

THE BIBLE SIN, MORALITY, JUDGEMENT AND FORGIVENESS

One of the key themes in the Scriptures, from Genesis to Revelation, is the issue of sin.

The 'Fact of Sin' - The 'Big Elephant in the Room'

> "And this is the condemnation, that
> light is come into the world,
> and **men loved darkness rather than
> light, because their deeds were evil**.
> For every one that does evil hates the
> light, neither comes to the light,
> lest his deeds should be reproved.
> But he that does truth comes to the light,
> that his deeds may be made manifest,
> that they are wrought in God."
> John 3:19-21

*Moreover, brethren, I declare unto you
the gospel which I preached to you,
which also you have received,
and wherein you stand;
By which also you are saved, if you keep
in memory what I preached to you,
unless you have believed in vain.
For I delivered to you first of all
that which I also received,
how that **Christ died for our sins
according to the Scriptures**;
And that He was buried, and that
He rose again the third day
according to the Scriptures."
1Corinthians 15:1-4*

Why is 'sin' such a big deal with God?

The simple answer to this commonly asked question is found in the fact that God is 'holy'. Therefore, He cannot allow sin with all it's effects, attitudes and destruction to exist in His presence.

Sin from God's view is "darkness", "evil", "perverted", "unnatural" and "unholy" and counter to His will.

It is God's divine love that will not allow Him to be passive about the destructive nature of sin on His children. This is why God has always explained to mankind what sin is throughout the Scriptures and why He has acted redemptively to "*save us from our sins*".

"And she shall bring forth a son, and
you shall call His name Jesus:
for ***He will save His people from their sins**.*"
Matthew 1:21

Who decides what is sin?

God is the only one who is qualified to determine what sin is. This is because of two of His divine attributes:-

Holiness - He is holy and knows what is holy and unholy, right and wrong

Justice - He is just and therefore cannot be unfair or unjust in any of His determinations

What is sin?

Sin is described in the Bible as the "*transgression of the law of God*".

"Whoever commits sin
transgresses also the law:
for sin is the transgression of the law."
1John 3:4

The law of God is very important because it reveals exactly what sin is and amplifies sin to "*become exceedingly sinful*". Therefore, we are all without excuse.

"Therefore the law is holy, and the
commandment holy and just and good.
Has then what is good become
death to me? Certainly not!
But sin, that it might appear sin, was producing
death in me through what is good;
so that sin through the commandment
might become exceedingly sinful."
Romans 7:12-13

The law and the Holy Scriptures define the boundaries and standards God has set for us and there can be no redefining, resetting, adjusting, minimizing, debating or omitting what God has clearly defined as sin.

Therefore all Bible-believing Christians are bound to the Scriptural definition of sin because God is the only one who can determine and define sin.

Sin Lists in the Scriptures

There are many '**sin lists**' in the Bible, which are too numerous to quote here. For the sake of space the following are the main lists of sins in the Bible.

The Old Testament Ten Commandments

"You will not have any other gods before me.
You will not make any graven image,
or any likeness of any thing
that is in heaven above,
or that is in the earth beneath, or that
is in the water under the earth.
You will not bow down to them, nor serve them:
for I the Lord your God am a jealous God,
visiting the iniquity of the
fathers upon the children
to the third and fourth generation
of them that hate me;
And showing mercy to thousands
of them that love me,
and keep my commandments.
You will not take the name of the
Lord your God in vain;
for the Lord will not hold him guiltless

that takes His name in vain.
Remember the sabbath day, to keep it holy.
Six days you will labour, and do all your work:
But the seventh day is the sabbath
of the Lord your God:
in it you will not do any work, nor your
son, nor your daughter, your manservant,
nor your maidservant, nor your cattle, nor
the stranger that is within your gates:
For in six days the Lord made heaven and
earth, the sea, and all that in them is,
and rested the seventh day:
therefore the Lord blessed the
sabbath day, and hallowed it.
Honor your father and mother:
that your days may be long upon the land
that the Lord your God gives you.
You will not kill.
You will not commit adultery.
You will not steal.
You will not bear false witness
against your neighbour.
You will not covet your neighbor's house,
you will not covet your neighbor's wife,
nor his manservant, nor his maidservant,
nor his ox, nor his ass,

nor any thing that is your neighbor's"
Exodus 20:4-17

The New Testament Sin Lists

"Because, although they knew God,
they did not glorify Him as God,
nor were thankful; but became
futile in their thoughts,
and their foolish hearts were darkened.
professing to be wise, they became fools,
And changed the glory of the incorruptible God
into an image made like
corruptible man - and birds,
and four-footed-animals, and creeping things.
Therefore, God also gave them up to
uncleanness, in the lusts of their hearts,
to dishonor their bodies among themselves:
who exchanged the truth of God for a lie,
and worshipped and served the
creature rather than the Creator,
who is blessed for ever. Amen.
For this reason God gave them
up to vile passions:
for even their women exchanged the
natural use for what is against nature:

*likewise also the men, leaving the
natural use of the woman,
burned in their lust for one another, men
with men committing what is shameful,
and receiving in themselves the penalty
of their error which was due.
And even as they did not like to
retain God in their knowledge,
God gave them over to a debased mind,
to do those things which are not fitting;
Being filled with all unrighteousness, sexual
immorality, wickedness, covetousness,
maliciousness; full of envy, murder,
strife, deceit, evil mindedness;
they are whisperers, backbiters, haters
of God, violent, proud, boasters,
inventors of evil things, disobedient to parents,
undiscerning, untrustworthy, unloving
unforgiving, unmerciful:
Who, knowing the righteous judgment of God,
that those who practice such things
are deserving of death,
not only do the same but also approve
of those who practice them."
Romans 1:21-32*

*"Do you not know that the unrighteous
shall not inherit the kingdom of God?
Be not deceived: neither fornicators,
nor idolaters, nor adulterers,
nor effeminate, nor homosexuals,
nor thieves, nor covetous,
nor drunkards, nor revilers, nor extortioners,
shall inherit the kingdom of God."
1Corinthians 6:9-10*

*"Now the works of the flesh are
manifest, which are these;
Adultery, fornication, uncleanness,
lasciviousness,
Idolatry, witchcraft, hatred, variance, emulations,
wrath, strife, seditions, heresies,
Envy, murders, drunkenness,
revelries, and the like:
of the which I tell you before, as I
have also told you in time past,
that they which do such things shall
not inherit the kingdom of God."
Galatians 5:19-21*

The Bible and the judgement of Sin

Wherever sin exists, God must judge sin because of His holy and just nature. God cannot act contrary to who He is and His divine attributes.

The Bible describes sin as falling short, or below, the glory of God.

> *"For all have sinned, and fallen*
> *short of the glory of God."*
> *Romans 3:23*

There must therefore be a penalty for sin because of Gods justice. That penalty is death which God declared at the fall of Adam and Eve and confirmed by the apostle Paul.

> *"And the Lord God commanded*
> *the man, saying,*
> *Of every tree of the garden you may freely eat:*
> *But of the tree of the knowledge of*
> *good and evil, you shalt not eat of it:*
> *for in the day that you eat of*
> *it you will surely die."*
> *Genesis 2:16-17*

"For the wages of sin is death."
Romans 6:23

The Bible and the Forgiveness of sin

As well as this judgement for sin, wherever it exists God will also forgive sin because of His loving, merciful and gracious nature. God cannot act contrary to who He is and His divine attributes.

The Bible describes the forgiveness of sin as an act of God's love, mercy and grace.

"In whom we have redemption through
his blood, the forgiveness of sins,
according to the riches of his grace."
Ephesians 1:7

God judges sin and forgives sin...at the same time

In our present, post modern culture, where "love is non-judging and inclusive ", it can be difficult for many to understand these two seemingly opposing aspects of God's nature.

That, at the same time that God judges sin, because He

is holy and just, He also forgives sin because He is loving and gracious.

> *"For the wages of sin is death*
> *but the gift of God is eternal life*
> *through Jesus Christ our Lord."*
> *Romans 6:23*

> *"But God, Who is rich in mercy, for His*
> *great love wherewith He loved us,*
> *Even when we were dead in sins,*
> *has quickened us together with*
> *Christ, (by grace you are saved;)*
> *And has raised us up together,*
> *and made us sit together in heavenly*
> *places in Christ Jesus:*
> *That in the ages to come He might show*
> *the exceeding riches of His grace*
> *in his kindness toward us through Christ Jesus.*
> *For by grace you are saved through*
> *faith; and that not of yourselves:*
> *it is the gift of God: Not of works,*
> *lest any man should boast."*
> *Ephesians 2:4-8*

The provision of forgiveness of sin for all who believe

The good news of the Gospel is that the Lord Jesus Christ died for the forgiveness of sins for the whole world. This forgiveness has been made available to "*all who believe*".

> *"And He [that same Jesus] is the*
> *propitiation for our sins*
> *[the atoning sacrifice that holds*
> *back the wrath of God*
> *that would otherwise be directed at us*
> *because of our sinful nature—our*
> *worldliness, our lifestyle];*
> *and not for ours alone, but also for [the*
> *sins of all believers throughout]*
> *the whole world."*
> *1John 2:2 Amplified Bible*

The personal and conscious decision of faith

It is through the personal and conscious decision to believe in the provision of Christ's forgiveness that we are justified and made righteous before God. This is how God forgives sin.

*"But now the righteousness of God
without the law is manifested,
being witnessed by the law and the prophets;
Even the righteousness of God
which is by faith of Jesus Christ
unto all and upon all them that believe:
for there is no difference."
Romans 3:21-22*

We are now justified with God by faith and live a life of peace and joy. We stand completely forgiven and justified as God's children in His very presence!

*"Therefore being justified by faith,
we have peace with God through
our Lord Jesus Christ:
By whom also we have access by faith
into this grace wherein we stand,
and rejoice in hope of the glory of God."
Romans 5:1-2*

CHAPTER SEVEN

THE APPLICATION OF THE BIBLE IN EVERY DAY LIFE

The Scriptures are central to the life and faith of every 'Bible-believing' Christian.

Without the Bible we have no moral compass, no certainty on how we should act and behave in this world. Trying to rely on our human thoughts, conscience or feelings alone, which are all fallible, can be so inaccurate when it comes to understanding eternal, spiritual matters.

So, what do we believe and practice in the Bible? How do we apply the Scriptures to our lives?

There are three levels of belief and practice for Christians in the Bible:-

"THE CORE" - **the specific, literal commands and**

requirements of Scripture. These are the '**Irreducible elements of our faith**', the non-negotiables. There is no need for interpretation or explanation because the command and requirement of the Scriptures are plain, simple to understand and literal.

Many Christians misunderstand the grace of God believing that because we are "under grace", the Old Testament law no longer applies to us. However, the grace of God does not do away with the law, it fulfills the law.

> *"Think not that I am come to destroy*
> *the law, or the prophets:*
> *I am not come to destroy, but to fulfill."*
> *Matthew 5:17*

The grace of God exceeds the requirements of the law by the power of the Holy Spirit working through faith in the believer! The "law and the prophets" witness this fact.

> *"But now the righteousness of God*
> *without the law is manifested,*
> *being witnessed by the law and the prophets;*
> *Even the righteousness of God*
> *which is by faith of Jesus Christ*

to all and upon all them who believe:
for there is no difference."
Romans 3:21-22

There are over 1000 commands and specific requirements in the New Testament.

Some examples of these 'Core' Scriptural commands and requirements are:-

- *"This is My commandment, that you love one another as I have loved you."* (John15:12; 1John 4:21)

- *"Let not sin reign in the body"* (Romans 6:12)

- *"Do not commit adultery"* (James 2:11)

- *"Let all bitterness, wrath, anger, clamor and evil speaking be put away from you."* (Ephesians 4:31)

- *"Let him who stole steal no longer"* (Ephesians 4:28)

- *"Do not be drunk with wine, in which is dissipation."* (Ephesians 5:18)

- *"For as often as you eat this bread and drink this cup, you proclaim the Lord's death until He comes."* (1Corinthians 11:26; Matthew 26:26-27)

- *"But if you do not forgive men their trespasses, neither will your Father forgive your trespasses."* (Matthew 6:15)

- *"Go therefore and make disciples of all nations, baptizing them in the name of the Father and of the Son and of the Holy Spirit."* (Matthew 28:19)

"**THE ESSENTIAL**" - **the interpretation of important principles, exhortations and standards of the Scriptures**. This is known as 'Hermeneutics', or Bible interpretation. For example, the gathering together as the church for worship and fellowship and includes exhortations and encouragements for Christians to do so in the Scriptures. For example the writer of Hebrews appeals to believers to not forsake gathering together as the church for worship and fellowship (Hebrews 10:25). Also, we read in the Book of Acts that the early church made gathering together in the temple and house to house a common and daily practice. This was done for teaching, fellowship, prayer, hospitality and praise (Acts 2:42,46-47). Therefore, gathering together as the church is considered an 'essential' practice for every Christian and has been so since the beginning of the church.

"THE NON-ESSENTIAL" - **the exercise of individual conscience and choice where there is no command or requirement of Scripture.** The right to exercise conscience is generally understood to exist where there are no specific commands ('Core') or standards ('Essentials') of Scripture. Furthermore, there are no 'eternal consequences' for practicing or non-practicing. For example, drinking alcohol, diet and food practices. *"But food does not commend us to God: for neither if we eat are we the better, nor if we do not eat are we the worse."* (1Corinthians 8:8)

Liberalism Versus Fundamentalism

Over the centuries Christians have oscillated between either a strict observance or a more liberal observance of the Scriptures. This has created two opposite views of the Scriptures, namely, Liberalism and Fundamentalism.

The essential difference between 'Liberalism' and 'Fundamentalism' is that '**Liberalism**' moves us from the 'Core' and 'Essential' to 'Conscience', producing '**license**'. In other words, we live as we personally feel, desire and think, regardless of any command or requirement of Scripture.

'**Fundamentalism**', on the other hand, moves us in the opposite direction from 'Conscience' to 'Essential' and 'Core', producing '**legalism**'. In other words, there is no individual conscience or choice, we live literally by every Scripture and by extension the 'commands' and practices of 'the church'.

When believers understand the distinction between what is 'core', what is 'essential' and what is 'conscience' a more balanced belief, attitude and lifestyle will emerge.

CHAPTER EIGHT

WHAT THE BIBLE WILL DO IN YOU AND FOR YOU

"For the Word of God is living and active and sharper than any double-edged sword, piercing even to the point of dividing soul from spirit, and joints from marrow; it is able to judge the desires and thoughts of the heart."
Hebrews 4:12 (NET Bible)

In His prayer in John chapter 17 Jesus declares to the Father that he has given his disciples:-

The **ETERNAL LIFE** of God (v3)

The **NAME** of the Father (v6)

The **JOY** of Christ (v13)

The **WORD** of God (v14-17)

The **GLORY** of God (v22)

Notice that the Word of God is included by Christ in His 'gifts' to the disciples and is therefore vital to our salvation and sanctification.

> *"**I have given them Your word**;*
> *and the world has hated them,*
> *because they are not of the world,*
> *even as I am not of the world.*
> *I pray not that you should take*
> *them out of the world*
> *but that You would keep them from the evil.*
> *They are not of the world, even*
> *as I am not of the world.*
> ***Sanctify them through Your***
> ***truth: Your word is truth**."*

In 17:14-17 Jesus outlined two responses in people to the Word of God:-

1. The Word of God causes a **REACTION** in those who **reject it** (John 17:14)

2. The Word of God **SANCTIFIES** those who **obey it** (John 17:6,14)

The Word of God possesses an inherent, supernatural power to cause change in the heart and life of the person who receives it by faith.

This ongoing change in us is called 'sanctification', which put simply, is the process of **SEPARATING, OR SETTING US APART, TO GOD.**

> *It is important to understand that the Word of God will change us as we embrace it by faith. "That you may be blameless and harmless, the sons of God, without rebuke, in the midst of a crooked and perverse generation, among whom you shine as lights in the world;* **Holding forth the word of life**..." *Philippians 2:14-16*

We are made different and make a difference for God in this world in direct proportion to our relationship with the Word of God

As disciples of Christ we are to be *"Holding forth the word of life"*, that is, "**OFFERING THE WORD OF LIFE TO ALL MEN**".

*"Holding out [to it] and offering [to
all men] the Word of Life..."
(Amplified Bible)*

We *"offer the Word of life"* through our changed lives, which become living examples, or *"shining lights"* in the darkness and chaos of this world.

We also *"offer the Word of life"* when we declare and present the Word of God to those around us.

But we can't do this by being the same as those around us! God's Word makes us different because we are called to be different and to make a difference.

This is what true discipleship is all about; allowing God to change us by believing and obeying the Word of God.

God's Word changes us on the inside and affects every area of our lives by 'removing the spirit of the world' from us.

*"Love not the world, neither the
things that are in the world.
If any man love the world, the love
of the Father is not in him.
For all that is in the world, **the lust of the flesh**,*

*and the **lust of the eyes**, and **the pride of life**,*
is not of the Father, but is of the world.
And the world passes away, and the lust thereof:
*but **he that does the will of***
***God abides for ever**.*
1John 2:15-17

"**The World**" that the apostle John was referring to was the "*kosmos*" (Strongs Concordance, G2889), or the '***worldly order of things***'.

This idea contains the concept of a 'worldly system and spirit' that is based on lust, desire and pride.

This 'system' of the world seduces us and draws us away from God and becomes the antithesis and the obstacle to the cause of Christ.

God wants to 'detox us', or 'sanctify us', from the "*things in the world*" which John described in 1John 2:16 as:-

"***the lust of the flesh***" = "*craving for sensual gratification*" (Amplified Bible)

"***the lust of the eyes***" = "*greedy longings of the mind*" (Amplified Bible) "**the pride of life**" = "*assurance in one's own resources or in the stability of earthly things*" (Amplified Bible)

In fact, the apostle John stated that "*these do not come from the Father but are from the world [itself]." (1John 2:16 Amplified Bible).*

God's Word changes us as we obey it

This 'sanctifying change' occurs in us through the word of God as we believe it and obey it.

Eighteen things the Word of God will do IN and FOR us

1. We are **BORN AGAIN** supernaturally by the Word of God

> "*Being born again, not of corruptible seed, but of **incorruptible (seed)**, **by the word of God**, which lives and abides for ever.*"
> *1Peter 1:23*

2. We will **GROW** spiritually by the Word of God

> "*As newborn babes, desire the*

*sincere milk of the **word**,*
that you may grow thereby."
1Peter 2:2

3. We will **FRAME OUR WORLDS,** or realities, by the Word of God

"Through faith we understand that
the worlds were framed by the word of God,
so that things which are seen were not
made of things which do appear."
Hebrews 11:3

4. We are made **COMPLETE** and **FULLY EQUIPPED** for every good work by the Word of God

*"**All Scripture** is given by inspiration of God,*
and is profitable for doctrine, for
reproof, for correction,
for instruction in righteousness:
*That the man of God may be **complete**,*
***throughly equipped for every good work**."*
2Timothy 3:16-17

5. We find a **MIRROR** to discover the blessed life by the Word of God

*"**But be sure you live out the message**
and do not merely listen to it and
so deceive yourselves.
For if someone merely listens to the
message and does not live it out,
he is like someone who **gazes at
his own face in a mirror**.
For he gazes at himself and then goes out
and immediately forgets what
sort of person he was.
But the one who peers into the
perfect law of liberty
and **fixes his attention there**,
and does not become a forgetful
listener **but one who lives it out
– he will be blessed in what he does."**
James 1:22-25 (NET)*

*"But we all, with unveiled face **beholding
as in a mirror the glory of the Lord**,
are **transformed into the same
image from glory to glory**,
even as from the Lord, the Spirit."
2Corinthians 3:18*

It is through the "*mirror*" of the word of God that we see ourselves as God sees us; transformed by the Spirit of God into His divine image and likeness!

This is the eternal plan of God and therefore the calling of every believer, to be conformed to the image of the Lord Jesus Christ.

"For whom He foreknew,
He also predestined to be conformed
to the image of His Son,
that He might be the firstborn
among many brethren."
Romans 8:29

This is because all who God is, and all that God possesses is vested in His Son, the Lord Jesus Christ.

"Has in these last days spoken to us by His Son,
whom He has appointed heir of all things,
through whom also He made the worlds;
Who being the brightness of His glory,
and the express image of His person,
and upholding all things by
the word of His power,
when He had by Himself purged our sins,
sat down at the right hand of
the Majesty on high…"
Hebrews 1:2-3

6. We discover God's **DIVINE HEALING AND DELIVERANCE** by the Word of God

*"He sent his **word**, and **healed** them,*

*and **delivered** them from their destructions"*
Psalm 107:20

7. We are **GUIDED** by the Word of God

*"Your **word** is a lamp to my feet,*
and a light to my path."
Psalm 119:105

8. We receive **COMFORT AND ENCOURAGEMENT** from the Word of God

"For whatever things were written
before were written for our learning,
*that we through patience and **comfort***
*of the **Scriptures** might have hope."*
Romans 15:4

9. We are made **WISE** unto salvation

"And that from a child you have
*known the **Holy Scriptures**,*
which are able to make you
wise unto salvation."
2Timothy 3:15

10. **FAITH** is produced in us

"But what does it say?
The word is near you, in your
mouth and in your heart
(that is, the word of faith, which we preach)…
*So then **faith comes by hearing, and***
***hearing by the word of God**."*
Rom 10:8,17

11. We receive **DOCTRINE** from the Word of God

*"**All Scripture** is given by inspiration of God,*
*and is profitable for **doctrine***
***(teaching - AMP)**…"*
2Timothy 3:16

12. We receive **REPROOF** from the Word of God

*"**All Scripture** is given by inspiration of God,*
*and is profitable for **reproof***
***(conviction - AMP)**…"*
2Timothy 3:16

13. We receive **CORRECTION** from the Word of God

*"**All Scripture** is given by inspiration of God,*
*and is profitable for **correction…**"*
2Timothy 3:16

14. We receive **INSTRUCTION** from the Word of God

*"**All Scripture** is given by inspiration of God,
and is profitable **instruction (training
- AMP)** in righteousness…"*

15. We receive the **PEACE** of God from the Word of God

*"Great peace have they who love Your law,
and nothing shall offend them."
Psalm 119:165*

16. We are endowed with **WISDOM** and **UNDERSTANDING** from the Word of God

*"You, through Your commandments,
make me wiser than my enemies:
for they are ever with me.
I have more understanding than all my teachers,
for Your testimonies are my meditation.
I understand more than the ancients,
because I keep Your precepts."
Psalm 119:98-100*

17. We are taught **HOW TO PRAY** by the Word of God

"And this is the confidence that we have in Him,

that if we ask any thing according
to his will, He hears us.
And if we know that he hears
us, whatever we ask,
we know that we have the petitions
that we have asked of Him."
1John 5:14-15

18. We are made **FRUITFUL** and **PROSPEROUS** by the Word of God

"But his delight is in the law of the Lord,
and in His law he meditates day and night.
He shall be like a tree planted
by the rivers of water,
that brings forth its fruit in its season,
Whose leaf also shall not wither;
and whatever he does shall prosper."
Psalm 1:1-3

CHAPTER NINE

LIVING DAILY IN THE SCRIPTURES

The Bible is not a book to be merely read. It is different to any other book because it is living and active. The Bible is a spiritual, supernatural book!

> *"For the word of God is alive and powerful,*
> *and sharper than any two edged sword,*
> *piercing even to the dividing asunder*
> *of soul and spirit, and of the joints*
> *and marrow, and is a discerner of the*
> *thoughts and intents of the heart."*
> *Hebrews 4:12*

Therefore, the Bible guides, inspires, empowers and transforms the believer when it is believed, trusted and acted upon in faith.

"For if anyone is a hearer of the
word and not a doer,
he is like a man observing his
natural face in a mirror;
For he observes himself, goes away,
and immediately forgets what
kind of man he was.
But he who looks into the perfect law
of liberty, and continues in it,
and is not a forgetful hearer,
but a doer of the work,
this one will be blessed in what he does."
James 1:23-25

Five ways to live daily in the Scriptures

1. READ the Scriptures

The Bible is a book to be read and consumed as often and as regularly as possible because it contains the divine life for all who believe. The best way to ensure this is by developing a regular and daily habit of reading the Scriptures.

"Till I come, give attention to reading,
to exhortation, to doctrine."
1Timothy 4:13

There are numerous read the Bible plans and helps available in 'APP' form which most people can access and these can be a great starting point to help believers form a daily habit of reading the Scriptures. However, I believe there is no substitute for physically reading your personal copy of the Bible.

The most simple way to start reading the Bible every day is to start at Genesis chapter one and Matthew chapter one and read a chapter a day from the Old and New Testaments.

Pray Reading

The prayerful reading, or praying as you read the Scriptures, is the foundation for living the Christian life.

Daily and regular '**pray reading**' of the Scriptures is spiritual food for the spiritual life of faith. This is because faith without the *"word of faith"* is simply positive thinking.

> *"So then faith comes by hearing, and hearing by the word of God."*
> *Romans 10:17*

When we prayerfully read the Scriptures we will find ourselves lifted from our need consciousness into the provisions and abundant supply of the living and powerful Word of God!

> ### *It is more important to 'pray reading' (the Scriptures), than to 'pray needing' (our needs list)!*

2. MEDITATE on the Scriptures

The Bible actually never teaches us to memorize the Scriptures, even though there can be some value in memorization.

However, the Bible does repeatedly and often say a lot about "**MEDIATING**" on the Word of God; "*day and night*".

> *"But his delight is in the law of the Lord;*
> *and in His law he **meditates** day and night."*
> *Psalm 1:2*

So, what is the difference between memorization and meditation?

"Memorization is the process of committing something to memory, this understanding and knowledge is acquired through rote memorization." (dictionary.com)

"Meditation is the act of thinking about something very carefully and deeply for a long time." (CED)

Meditation is more than the rote, or parrot like, memorization of the Scriptures. It goes far deeper than just desiring to recall or quote the Bible.

Meditation is the regular practice and habit of focusing the mind and heart on a particular Scripture for a long time.

This technique increases the awareness of the person meditating so they can receive spiritual inspiration, revelation, understanding and knowledge from the Holy Spirit about a particular Scripture.

It is through the practice of regular and prayerful meditation in the Scriptures that the Holy Spirit is given time and the greater opportunity to lead, guide and reveal the things of God to the believer.

"But God has revealed them to us by His Spirit:
for the Spirit searches all things,

yes, the deep things of God.
Now we have received, not the spirit of the
world, but the Spirit who is from God;
that we might know the things that
are freely given to us by God."
1Corinthians 2:10,12

3. CONFESS the Scriptures

It is common to think of the concept of confession only in terms of the confession of sin.

However, the confession of the Scriptures is far more broader and includes the verbal confessing, stating, acknowledging and affirming of the promises of God's Word.

"This book of the law shall not
depart out of your mouth;
but you shall meditate in it day and night,
that you may observe to do according
to all that is written therein:
for then you will make your way prosperous,
and then you will have good success."
Joshua 1:8

The apostle Paul encouraged Philemon that by *"acknowledging all the good things that are in you in Christ Jesus"* he would possess an *"effective communication of faith"*.

> *"That the communication of thy*
> *faith may become effective*
> *by the acknowledging of every good*
> *thing which is in you in Christ Jesus."*
> *Philemon 6*

The Word of God, or *"word of faith"*, is near us because it is *"believed in our hearts"* and *"confessed in our mouths"*.

> *"But what does it say?*
> *The word is near you, even **in your***
> ***mouth**, and **in your heart**:*
> *that is, **the word of faith**, which we preach."*
> *Romans 10:10*

The personal, daily and consistent verbal confession of the promises of God given to us in the Scriptures will lead us to possess them.

> *"And Jesus answered them, Have faith in God.*
> *For truly I say to you, That whoever*

*shall **say** to this mountain,*
Be removed, and be cast into the sea;
and shall not doubt in his heart,
but shall believe that those things
*which he **says** shall come to pass;*
*he shall have whatever he **says**."*
Mark 11:22-23

Just as faith without works is dead,
So faith without words is dead!

4. STUDY the Scriptures

To move beyond the basics and foundations of our faith, the Scriptures instruct us to study, or dig deeper into the Word of God.

"Study to show yourself approved to God,
a workman that does not need to be ashamed,
rightly dividing the word of truth."
2Timothy 2:15

Study occurs when we move from reading and meditating on the Scriptures to searching, enquiring, investigating and researching the Scriptures.

When we do this we will discover answers to our questions, develop a broader understanding of the truths in the Scriptures and receive revelation and guidance from the Holy Spirit, who *"leads us in all truth"*.

Ways to Study the Bible

Study Books of the Bible

We can study books of the Bible by covering key verses, key words and phrases, topics of doctrine.

Take for example the book of Romans.

a. Key theme - Salvation

The Condition (Chapter 1-2) - The lost state of men

The Answer (Chapter 3) - Justification by faith

The Example (Chapter 4) - Abraham

The Blessings of Salvation (chapter 5)

The Results (Chapter 6&7) - Part 1 - the Old Life Left

The Results (Chapter 8) - Part 2 - The New Life Begun

b. Characters studies

Christ as the Key to the whole Bible

Gideon - leadership, guidance, God's way of fighting

Abraham - father of faith

Ruth - faithfulness and redemption

David and Saul - spiritual versus carnal man

c. Subjects and Doctrine study

Salvation

Redemption

Sanctification

Faith

Money

Healing

d. Word studies - Key words and phrases throughout the Bible

"The way"	"The truth"	"The life"
"Light"	"Love"	"Life"

5. PRACTICE the Scriptures

As we read, meditate, confess and study the Scriptures we discover the depth and breadth of the promises of God's Word. We learn that every area of our lives are provided for through the promises of God.

> *"According as his divine power*
> *has given unto us all things*
> *that pertain to life and godliness,*
> *through the knowledge of Him who*
> *has called us to glory and virtue.*
> *Whereby are given unto us exceeding*
> *great and precious promises:*
> *that by these you might be*
> *partakers of the divine nature,*
> *having escaped the corruption that*
> *is in the world through lust."*
> *2Peter 1:3-4*

Why are the provisions of Christ presented to us in the form of promises?

Because we are called to "*live by faith*".

Therefore, it is through the application and practice of the promises of God in our lives through faith that we partake and experience the "divine nature", because, *"faith without works is dead"*! *(James 2:17).*

Applying the promises of God to our needs

The most applicable way to exercise faith in the promises of God is to apply a particular promise of God to a particular need, lack or challenge in our lives.

For example

If I am sick and unwell, the promise of God is that Jesus Christ is my healing and health.

> *"Who his own self bare our sins in his*
> *own body on the tree, that we,*
> *being dead to sins, should live*
> *unto righteousness:*
> *by whose stripes you were healed."*
> *1Peter 2:24*

If I am facing challenging and difficult circumstances, the promise of God is that Jesus Christ is my strength and enabler in every situation.

> *"I can do all things through Christ*
> *who strengthens me."*
> *Philippians 4:13*

If I have experienced loss in my life, the promise of God is that Jesus Christ is my comfort and able to make every bad situation work out for good.

*"And we know that all things work together
for good to them who love God,
to those who are the called
according to his purpose."*
Romans 8:28

Note: Time and space will not allow us to cover all of the more than **8,000 promises** contained in the Bible!

Always Pray to God based on the promises of God

Once we have identified a specific promise in God's Word regarding a specific need in our life, then we can pray to God based on the promise of God. This is the power of the prayer of faith in action that is aligned with God's will.

*"Is anyone among you sick? Let him
call for the elders of the church,
and let them pray over him, anointing
him with oil in the name of the Lord:
And the prayer of faith will save the
sick, and the Lord will raise him up.
And if he has committed sins,
he will be forgiven."*
James 5:14-15

Praying the promises of God is praying according to God's will

"Now this is the confidence that we have in Him,
that if we ask anything according
to His will, He hears us.
And if we know that He hears us,
we know that we have the petitions
that we have asked of Him."
1John 4:14-15

BIBLIOGRAPHY

Josh McDowell - josh.com

biblearcheologyreport.com

www.csntm.org

britannia.com

The Thompson Chain Reference Bible

"1050 New Testament Commands", www.abc.net.au

www.tertullian.org resources

www.gracelifebiblechurch.com resources

www.christianpublishinghouse.com

www.winterparkcocnc.com resources

*"FOREVER, O LORD,
YOUR WORD IS SETTLED IN HEAVEN."*
Psalm 119:89

DR GORDON MOORE

BOOKS

AVAILABLE AMAZON & KINDLE

INFO@THELIGHTHOUSE.CHURCH

NORMAL CHRISTIANITY
LIVING IN THE PROVISIONS OF THE CROSS OF CHRIST

GORDON MOORE

GOD OF *miracles*

GORDON MOORE

Yes HOLY SPIRIT

GORDON MOORE

GOING TO THE NEXT LEVEL

TAKE SOMEONE WITH YOU

GORDON MOORE

LEADERSHIP STYLES & LEVELS OF CHURCH

CHURCH
GATE OF HEAVEN

GORDON MOORE

BLENDED families

GORDON MOORE

ASCENT

GORDON MOORE

9 7 8 1 7 6 3 6 4 6 8 9 6